The Pain of My Inheritance:

My Mother's Wound

Sabrina J. Robertson

Dedication

Praise be to God who ALWAYS causes us to triumph! 2 Corinthians 2:14

This book is dedicated my daughters Carjonie who bore the pain of my inherited wounds long before I even realized I was injured & LaShara who trusted me to be a part of her healing process. And to my Grand Prince, my Sweet Baby Ray & my Grand Doll, Nahla Jonel from the moment you were born until the moment I die, everything I do, will be for you!

Acknowledgements

As I sit in the realness of this moment that both starts and ends with MY Lord and Savior, Jesus Christ I suddenly feel at a loss for words that will accurately describe how his unfailing love for me saved my life. For the many dark nights that I waged war with weapons that were not carnal to the rainy days that saw my mourning transformed to dancing! I give you Praise because YOU are a Good, Good father and I without a doubt am not lucky...I'm loved!

To my Big Sisters Charlotte & Andrea: I honor you for the childhood and adolescence you sacrificed to cover me. I honor you for pushing me to go further when I decided I was through. I honor you for a lifetime of being willing and committed to hurting those who hurt me. I honor you for loving me when those who were supposed to...simply couldn't. I honor you.

I knew when I started this that if I started to name names someone would undoubtedly be left out so I'm asking in advance if you're scanning this, looking for your name if you find it absent, please charge it to my head and not my heart.

To Angie, Kristi & Delana: There would be no me without you! No matter what, whenever, however, where ever my heart always is and always will be with you.

To My Graces: Dionne, Demetrianna (Dede), Tania & ReVonda: God literally used you all to save me life!! From contemplating who would find me if I swallowed a bottle of pills to life MORE abundantly you all literally picked me up and showed me HOW to live again.

To my sisters AKA "The Cut-Up Crew" Montreece, Benita & Rhonda: "If doing life together" was a garment we ALWAYS wear it well! Greater is coming & we're going after it together!

To the LADIES of Rage: Thank you Sisters for nearly 20 years of gaining enlightenment through shared pain, tears, laughter, joy, triumphs and even sorrow! Here's to another 20 years!!

To My Personal Rabbi Dr. William H. Coleman III & My Only Lady Dionne Coleman: Thank you for ALWAYS being there, supporting, holding and allowing me to be me.

To my mother Gwen Cagler: Thank you for enduring all that you did. Thank you for never giving up. But most of all Thank you for surviving! I Love you.

And last but certainly not least, To My "Mom" Justine Miles: Thank you for taking someone else's daughter and loving her as your own! You set the standard for love without reason. When I think of you, I am convinced that God had you in mind when he breathed the inspiration for 1 Corinthians 13. Because of you I am happy, healthy, whole and ABLE. Able to Love. Able to Mother and able to breathe. I LOVE YOU.

Foreword

I met Sabrina Robertson about seven years ago on an incredible prayer line called Declare Victory. I instantly knew that there was something special about this woman! Her articulate manner of speech, wisdom and quick wit, made everyone stop and listen every time she opened her mouth. Because of her excellent hosting ability and eloquence of speech, we lovingly called her Vanna! She is a phenomenal sister friend who is passionate about helping people to heal, to hope and to dream.

Healing often begins with a self-examination of our lives to determine how we ended up in the place we now find ourselves in; the place where we use dysfunctional coping mechanisms to mask or process our painful lives. Low self- esteem, never feeling good enough, the inability to relate to others, and insecurities often stems from wounds that have been buried deep within. As a health care professional for over 20 years, I have seen many people struggle physically, mentally, and emotionally with unacknowledged or unresolved pain from their past. Many women suffer in silence believing the lies that they will never be healed. As a result, we teach our daughters, nieces, sisters and other women in our lives, how-to live-in dysfunction. It is often difficult to do the work of healing without the help of a compassionate person who has done or is doing the work themselves.

Sabrina is dedicated to walking you through the process of uncovering the sources of your pain! This book holds the revelation that the source of your pain may be closer to you than you think! It is intentionally written so that you and the women in your life can become healed, delivered, and set free from the pain of your past!

I am excited that Sabrina has put her God given wisdom in this book and I am doubly excited about your journey towards healing as you become the amazing person God created you to be!

Lisa R. Porter

One day Jesus came to Jerusalem and visited a popular bath house where many sick persons would lay waiting for something to happen to the waters of the pool. The understanding was, when the waters would begin to bubble the 1st person to get in would be healed of their affliction. As if He had an appointment, Jesus walks up to a man who'd been in his sickness for 38yrs – longer than the lifetime of most men in Jesus' day! Fastening His attention on the incapacitated man, Jesus asks him a very interesting, insightful yet simple question.... "Do you want to get well?" John 5:6b GNT

This seems an odd question to ask someone who's been sick for such a long period of time, yet Jesus thought it a good question to ask! Many have speculated as to why Jesus would ask such a question, but I think two things are obvious...It got the man's undivided attention, and it engaged his WILL! Jesus does not begin with a diagnostic analysis, a psychological evaluation or a DSM diagnosis! He begins with the most basic of human motivations – The Will

Before you go further into this book. Pause here, and allow Jesus to ask you... "Do you want to get well?" Sabrina Robertson has not simply written a book for the purpose of consumption, but with the love of a mother and the skill of a surgeon, Sabrina has crafted a tool that has the capacity to deliver deep healing for persons who, like this man, have been in their condition for a very long time! However, the key to it all is the WILL! Do you want to get well?

This is not a book that has come out of thin air. Even though Sabrina has the educational background, the mental capacity and the depth of knowledge to write such a book, this book is born out of a combination of education, intelligence and experience. In answer to the question, Do you want to get well? I have heard Sabrina say, "Yes"! I have watched the principles within this book come alive in her own journey of healing and wholeness. I have watched her hurt, trip, fall, heal, grow and develop into a person whose heart is like the heart of our Savior, who now shows up to your pool, in the middle of your pain, and dares to ask the question – Do you want to get well?

(Please answer before moving forward)

Yes   No   Not Sure

Q. Why is this part important? Why do I have to answer the question when all I want to do is read the book?

A. This is not just a book, it's a WORKbook!

Most healing is not an instantaneous proposition, but one of process! In the Biblical story of Naaman the Syrian general, he was sent to the prophet Elisha to be healed of his leprosy. Elisha instructs

12

him to wash himself 7 times in the Jordan river. Watch Naaman's response:

2 Kings 5:11 - 11 But Naaman went away angry and said, "I thought that he would surely come out to me and stand and call on the name of the Lord his God, wave his hand over the spot and cure me of my leprosy. NIV

Naaman wasn't expecting to do any work or have any part in his own healing, but this is contrary to how healing actually works. If we are going to be healed, it is going to be a combination of your will, this book and God's infinite grace! The acquiescence to do the work required reveals the will of the individual! In my Sabrina Robertson voice, I ask... "Do you want to get well?"

Pastor William H. Coleman III

Table of Contents

Introduction

Who are you? No really, who are you? When you show up in the world, out in the marketplace, in the lives of your loved ones and friends Who are you? When you look in the mirror who are you? Are you the sum total of your experiences, the wins and the loses? Are you who society and culture has convinced you to believe a "real" man, or a "real" woman is? Are you thriving or barely surviving? Do you feel stuck with no real idea why? Are you unable to answer these questions, hesitant to go deeper but tired of living on the surface? Tired of being frustrated, stagnated, guarded, and withdrawn for seemingly no identifiable reason at all? Do you desire to live the abundant life often preached about but never aimed for because you are unable to forge meaningful connections sustained in trust, value, and accountability?

Let me to put your mind at ease, you're not alone; in fact, YOU may not even be the cause of where you are right now! Well, you might be the cause of the symptoms but not the root! As I take a step back to let you off the hot seat as your mind swirls around the task of identifying your identity, let me encourage you to go back! Go back to your beginning, beyond your origin and past your inception; to fully grasp where you are, how you are and why you are you have to go back to where it all begin... a place whose location may be found generations before you even got here. It may take you quite the journey to get there but one you arrive, catch your breath take off your shoes and your coat and then ask yourself this final question: "Am I **THE** living, breathing, walking replication of the wounds of my mother?"

Selah

(Pause and calmly think about that)

In ‑her ‑it /inˈherət/

Verb: receive (money, property, or a title) as an heir at the death of the previous holder.

"She inherited a fortune from her father."

I don't know a parent that doesn't think about leaving an inheritance for their children, even if they aren't able to execute it, every well-intentioned parent holds a desire to leave their children with something lasting, tangible and defining. Whether it's property, land, wealth, riches, fortune, affluence, or access to education. For most parents, that desire is one of the driving forces for pursuit of career goals and success as it takes great focus, hard work and sacrifice to build a foundation that will sustain present, coming, and future generations. When we think about inheritances, we think about the respectable things; the objects and qualities people highlight during award shows, the things captured in magazine articles and feel-good stories. You know, those things that sometimes makes others just a little envious as they look at our lives, families and children and subtly wish to be in a pair of shoes just like ours.

It goes without saying, that the right inheritance can turn your whole life around! With the final closing of the right pair eyes or a stroke from the right pen many have gone from rags to riches within varying moments of the same day! When managed properly, the right kind of inheritance has the potential to secure the future of the beneficiary AND their descendants. The right kind of inheritance has the ability to offer access to freedoms and opportunities one otherwise may never know. That's the right kind of inheritance...but what about the wrong kind of inheritance?

Os·mo·sis /äzˈmōsəs,äsˈmōsəs
Noun

1. The process of gradual or unconscious assimilation of ideas, knowledge, etc.
2. "what she knows of the blue-blood set she learned not through birthright, not even through wealth, but through osmosis"
3. A passive transport of a solvent or material that does not require energy to be applied.

Have you ever experienced meeting someone and knowing right away prior to any introductions who their relatives were? Maybe it was based on a strong physical feature or characteristic, or maybe it was a distinguishing laugh or a trademark gait or perhaps it was a uniquely shaped dimple; whatever it is was you were able to make a positive association and identification back to that person's family of origin based solely on what you saw. As people, we sometimes tend to make the same types of associations with KNOWN negative patterns of behavior and characteristics which we package and call Generational Pathologies, Patterns and sometimes even Curses. Have you ever stopped to ponder where those things come from? Why they exist? And why they seem to plaque individuals of the same bloodline (even if it doesn't present in quite the same way)?

Substance use, promiscuity, mental health issues, gambling (and other forms of addictions), self-injurious behaviors and attitudes, emotional instability and the list can go on and on. My point is, like everything else in life, it has an origin and a root that can be steeped in generations that existed long before we were ever born leaving us vulnerable to prototypes and fates that without intervention can feel as if they are beyond our control.

IDENTIFYING THE MOTHER WOUND <u>IN ME</u>

"Healing beings where the wound was made".

Alice Walker

Mother Wounds are traumas that pass from one generation to the next. These are wounds that the generations before us failed to heal. These wounds often consist of toxic and dysfunctional systems comprised of oppressive beliefs, ideas, perceptions, and choices

You may suffer some level of mother-wounding if you:

- Find it easier to shut down than to express yourself
- Lie to protect others from your truth
- Don't trust yourself
- Feel disconnected from your natural intuition
- Long for validation from others
- Experienced as a child love conditionally based on your behavior
- As a child had love withheld until you met certain requirements
- Experience frequent fight or flight emotions
- Suffer from a consistent inability to securely attach within the confines of intimate relationships
- Experience frequent bouts of anxiety/depression

- Currently have or have had an eating disorder
- Have/Had a mother who rages, sulks, punishes, guilt's, practices silent treatment, and/or shames
- Have/Had a mother with borderline personality disorder, addiction and/or mental illness
- Have/Had a mother who wasn't acknowledged or validated for her sacrifices or care of the family
- Have/Had a disempowered mother or father
- As a child sought to carry your mother's pain for her
- Have/Had a jealous or resentful mother
- Wanted to "take care of" your mother
- Don't want to make mother "feel bad"
- Yearn for mother's approval, acknowledgement, appreciation, unconditional love
- Have/Had a mother who withholds love or loving words to prove a point or manipulate
- Have/Had a mother who intentionally injured you (mentally, physically or emotionally)
- Become tense and/or anxious when spending time with your mother
- Have ever made choices against your well-being to avoid upsetting mom, triggering her or to avoid conflict
- Have/Had a mother who criticizes, nags, nit-picks, fault-finds
- Do not feel appreciated, seen and/or heard by your mother

- Have/Had a sense that your mother wants (or wanted) to do a better job of acknowledging your awesomeness, but lacks the verbal skills or has limits around her capacity to honor you
- Have/Had a mother who has not grieved her losses or feels she has not lived up to her potential
- Have/Had a mother who displaced her feelings and/or projects onto you and/or still does
- Sense an unofficial agreement that you are not to surpass her in virtue, glory or accomplishment
- Have/Had a mother who competes with you or seeks to "one-up" you
- Have/Had a mother who dominates conversations or seems needy for your time, energy and approval
- Have/Had a mother with Narcissistic tendencies
- Have/Had a mother who competes with other women
- Experienced a mother who was/is energy-depleted or suffers from auto-immune disorder
- Have/Had a mother who had a fractured relationship with her mother
- Are not/Was not safe to express your feelings to your mother, or were not safe to do so as a child
- Have/Had a mother who relies on you for emotional support

- Have/Had a mother who does not have authentic friends or community
- Have/Had a mother who "knows best" or claims she knows you better than you know yourself
- Fear abandonment/rejection by mother
- Fear abandonment and/or rejection in your primary relationships, especially significant other
- Seldom feel "good enough"
- Tendency to self-sabotage your own efforts before they come to fruition
- Have/Had a mother who suffered sexual abuse, objectification or mental/physical/spiritual abuse as a child herself
- Consider yourself a "rescuer", "fixer" or "manager" of the family
- Consider yourself a "People Pleaser"
- Have/Had a wounded mother who has not healed her trauma/doesn't speak of it

Before we go any further, I want to stop and honor you for coming this far. To open yourself up to the awareness that there is something bubbling beneath the surface and to be willing to come face-to-face with it can be both courageous and scary. You may be asking, "So now what? Where do I go from here?" I'm glad you asked! Have you ever found yourself faced with a problem that appeared to be so massive that you got so overwhelmed that instead of doing something, anything even you just sat and did nothing? I've been there countless times myself! I remember one particular time I'd gotten so frustrated with wanting change but having no clue as to how to even get started that I turned to a mentor for advice on getting started. But instead of giving me the answer or solution to solve all of my problems, he looked at me with a question of his own and said, "Sabrina, how do you eat and elephant"? Frustrated, emotionally drained and not in the mood for a parable or a riddle I felt myself beginning to shut down on the inside as I began to think, if he didn't want to help me all he had to do was say so! Sensing my dejection, with compassion in his eyes, my mentor looked at me and said, "One bite at a time. That's how you eat an elephant Sabrina, one bite at a time". In other words, pick a starting place and dig in!

So that my friend is where we are headed; the next stop on this journey is where we will actually begin "Doing the work". Doing the work is a term that you will see and hear frequently throughout this workbook and while the term has become very cliché in our culture it's an actual thing! It's a series of actions or steps taken with the intentional focus of understanding yourself and what has shaped you. It is the process of understanding your flaws and how your emotions can cloud your ability to think and to act rationally. Finally, it is the action of introspection with self -awareness and the personal commitment of changing for the better.

Benefits of "Doing the Work:

- **Alleviation of depression:** Doing the work affords us the opportunity to find resolution and even happiness in situations that were once debilitating and stagnating.
- **Decreased stress:** Completing the process opens the door for us to live life with less anxiety and fear of things that we've experienced and survived.
- **Improved relationships:** Doing the work frees us to experience deeper connections and intimacy with the people we love and ourselves.
- **Reduced anger:** Doing the work helps us understand the root of our anger and resentment, giving us the power to become less reactive, restoring a greater sense of self-control and self-regulation.
- **Increased mental clarity:** Doing the work comes with the increased ability to live and work more intelligently and effectively with integrity.
- **More energy:** Doing the work produces a new sense of hope, optimism, resilience and determination.
- **More peace:** Completing the work produces a greater sense of self-awareness, self-acceptance and a healthy sense of positive self-esteem.

So, take a deep breath and let's get started!

This workbook has been spiritually inspired to guide you through a process of healing and restoration using the following six tenants and biblical principles based upon God's explicit desire for your life.

- Acknowledgment
- Identification
- Exploration
- Processing
- Intentional Decision Making
- Positive Forward Momentum

Acknowledgment – Every child needs four basic things: Acceptance, focused attention, guidance and protection. As a result of life circumstances those things may not always be readily available and consistent. We now know that the prolonged absence of these key provisions can result in many areas of deficits and impairments across the developmental landscape. And while it may feel like all hope is lost for the child left without these forms of nurturing Psalms 27: 7-14 assures us that we can turn to God to get all four of these emotional needs met.

The fear of reliving trauma and abuse keeps most victims from bringing up the depth of their experiences and understandably so. However, we cannot heal what we're reluctant to see. The notion that memories and residue of our past negative experiences will simply go away if we can successfully avoid thinking about them or bringing them up robs us of opportunities to be whole and leaves us vulnerable to being triggered by unsuspecting people who have no idea that we're wounded and hurt.

I often talk about the definition of insanity, doing the same thing over and over again while expecting a different result because trauma has a way of trapping us in cycle. And while on the surface it may appear that we're function just fine the truth is, if we're honest most of the time we're merely surviving as opposed to thriving. In a blog post on emotional wounding Author Melany Olive lists the following three ways we avoid our Emotional Wounds:

1. Making (keeping) ourselves busy
2. Intellectualizing (justifying) our patterns
3. Exaggerating our detachment (from the people and things that have hurt us)

Identification - The first thing we need to do is identify the problem and realize our need for inner healing. Below is a list of symptoms that commonly occur in people who have emotional wounding:

Emotional tenderness: The continued presence of a pain that never quite goes away even when you can't quite identify, explain or describe it.

Irritability: You become easily agitated with others even if they aren't doing anything wrong! You can see it happening and you may even hate it but, in that moment, you feel powerless to stop the way you're feeling, thinking or behaving.

Little to no tolerance: You may find that you have a low tolerance for anything other than having your desires an expectation met, even when they aren't reasonable and place others at a disadvantage.

Inability to regulate unhelpful negative emotions: Feelings of anger, hate, resentment, etc. seem to "rise up" within you at the slightest offense (perceived or valid) from others.

Extreme sensitivity about an event or events in your past: If there are events in your past which cause you to become very sensitive or angry, or even cause you to lash out, it is likely revealing a deep emotional wound tied in with that event or memory.

Inability or unwillingness to offer forgiveness and acceptance: It becomes very difficult, if not impossible to love and therefore forgive others. It can also be hard to forgive and love yourself. You may even find yourself feeling those same negative emotions towards God, feeling as if even he has hurt, offended or abandoned you.

Blinded to true authentic, sincere love: It is hard to clearly see and realize the love of others and God in your life. You may be surrounded by people who love you, but it can be difficult to fully feel and receive that love when you are emotionally wounded. There seems to be a wall up that blocks the flow of love into your life.

Lashing out: When there's an inner wound that has festered, it becomes easy to lash out or have sudden outbursts of anger, hate, resentment, etc. You may find it easy to lash out at people who love you and have done you no harm. Just like hurt people, hurt other people; wounded people sometimes and without intention wound other people.

Feelings of anger towards God: When a person has been wounded, it becomes easy to blame God for their troubles and hardships. This is the last thing that you want to do when seeking to be healed, because it virtually puts up a wall in your mind that can block the healing power of the Holy Spirit from operating. Although He desires to heal your wound, He will not override your freewill, and if you hold hate in your heart against Him, it can block his efforts to heal your wounds.

Self-hate: Many times, when a person is hurt from past abuse, they will begin to think that perhaps what happened to them, was deserved because of something they did or the way that they were. This is not true. Abuse is never acceptable, even if a child was misbehaving. Parental love disciplines and corrects, but never abuses.

Easily frustrated: Unpackaged emotional wounds have the ability to nurture a quiet storm of turmoil and emotions within us that can leave us vulnerable to becoming easily frustrated with ourselves, those around us and everyday chores & responsibilities. If you find yourself easily frustrated and always needing to take a breath and count to 10 that may be a sign that something is brewing beneath the surface.

The urge to escape: The torment from housing a constant narrative of emotional turmoil leaves us vulnerable to seeking out alternative methods of treatment such as self-medication through harmful actions, patterns and behaviors. As a result of inner turmoil, it is easy to desire to escape or suppress reality. This can be in the form of overeating, drinking, smoking, porn, spending binges, etc. When a person indulges in escapism, addictions can easily form.

Retaliation urges: Those with festering inner wounds and pint-up anger and hurt will find it easy to retaliate or snap back at people who offend them or step on their toes.

Self-sabotaging behavior: Inner pain has a way of consuming a person's mind, and eventually this can take on a careless approach to life. It's hard to value and feel good about yourself if you have an inner wound. If you don't feel good about yourself, it will begin to show in your lifestyle and communication.

Irrational & unreasonable expectations of others: Somebody who has been wounded may set high expectations for those around them. They may feel that others ought to live up to standards that even they themselves are unable to uphold and they can be very intolerable to any sort of mistakes made. They may find it particularly difficult to forbear (put up with) one another as the Bible commands of us (see Colossians 3:13).

Perfectionism: A person who has an emotional wound may also be performance driven. Perhaps they felt like no matter what they did, they could never please a parent or authority figure, and later on in life, that rejection wound causes the person to be a performer to the point where they are never satisfied only burnt out by their efforts.

Feelings of hopelessness: A profound loss of hope is a common result of unresolved inner wounds. Since the love of God is blocked in your life, it becomes hard to see why He would love or care for you, and therefore you become an easy target for feelings of hopelessness and despair.

Overdrive: When you suffer from emotional wounding, it can create a sense of void in your life's meaning, thus driving you to find meaning, purpose and happiness in things. This could be in the form of college degrees, careers, financial success, etc. Instead of appreciating the person who God created you to be, you find yourself chasing what you think will bring true happiness and purpose to your life.

Hostility towards God, self, and others: because of bound up emotions, a person can tend to feel hostile towards God, other people in their life and even themselves. This is usually rooted in a form of bitterness against God for not preventing something from happening to you, bitterness against somebody who has wronged or harmed you emotionally, or bitterness against yourself for failures that you yourself haven fallen into.

Exploration - Trauma generates negative emotions; unless we process these emotions at the time the trauma occurs, they become stuck in our minds **AND** in our bodies. Instead of healing from the wounding event, the trauma stays in our body as energy in our unconscious minds, affecting our lives until we uncover it and process it out. Processing distressing emotions like anger, sadness, shame, and fear, is essential to healing from trauma.

The healthiest and best way to respond to emotional wounding is also the rarest: Ideally, when the trauma first occurs, we should recognize the violation, allow ourselves to feel the natural emotions that follow, and then internalize the knowing that the violation doesn't say anything about us personally; doing that would make it easier to avoid the natural tendency to own responsibility (in part or in total) for the violation against us, thus freeing us to let the violation go and move forward.

Now that's what should happen, but the reality is emotions like anger and sadness are painful — and because crying or confronting others is uncomfortable and often times not socially acceptable it's a process that we run from as opposed to towards. Commonly we do this by suppressing our emotions, rather than giving ourselves permission to feel them in a healthy way. As a child, this process is even more difficult. What can feel like a pinprick to an adult, rude words or a dismissive attitude can feel like a stab wound to a child and create lasting damage both internally and externally.

Processing emotions in a healthy way means holding tight to the reality that emotions are temporary and fleeting. It means embracing the knowing that all emotions have a predictable beginning, middle, and end, and that no matter what it feels like in the moment we will survive. When we don't learn how to *feel* our feelings, we may start to interpret all emotions as being terrifying which will lead to a fear of feeling anything at all.

So, when uncomfortable emotions tied to negative memories come up sit with them and their sensations, let the feelings come up and flow organically. Don't try to change or hide them; pay attention to them. Acknowledge and welcome any discomfort you feel, knowing it will be gone soon and will help you to heal. Let your body respond the way it wants or needs to. If you feel the urge to cry, cry. If you feel the need to yell something or punch something, you should yell or punch the air. If you feel the urge to write, write. Expressing your emotions in a productive way is key to getting them moving inside you and ultimately through and out of you.

Processing - Emotional processing is the ability to process stress and other extreme events and move past them. When people are unable to process those emotions, they become susceptible to developing phobias and other disorders of mental health that they may otherwise not have been vulnerable to. Emotional processing allows specific and intense feelings to dissipate over time.

Intentional Decision making - As a result of our human construct often times we make decisions from a place of obligation, a perceived sense of responsibility, guilt or habit. When we live our lives based on decisions made from that place, we inadvertently resign ourselves to a life that is less rich, less vibrant and less than we were intended to live. In John 10:10 Jesus talks about his intention for us to live a life of abundance; the decisions we make can absolutely affect our ability to move into that space and stay there! When it comes to processing memories and emotions tied to past pain and trauma intentional decision making provides us with the ability to choose healing and recovery over a life resigned to pain and un-forgiveness.

Positive Forward Momentum - Sometimes life gives us a wake-up call, with the purpose of lighting a fire under our butts so that we will take action. The truth of the matter is, when it comes to making positive changes in our lives, though it may feel like we've been saddled with the force of a thousand weights the only thing holding us back from moving forward is ourselves. Change is hard in both theory and in practice! Sometimes it can feel better and safer to stay rooted in current circumstances simply because it's familiar and known. Diving head first into foreign waters of unchartered territory when you aren't even sure you know how to swim can seem crazy and courageous! But the reality is if you never take the leap, you'll never know just how far you can soar or how sweet living life more abundantly can be.

So, if you can honestly admit that you're tired of living the very definition of insanity, doing the same thing over and over again while expecting a different result and you're ready to take the largest leap you've ever taken towards emotional wealth, health and freedom; what are you waiting for my dear?? Take my hand and let's gooooo!!!!

Week One

❦ ❦ ♡ ❦ ❦

Grasping the Power to Overcome

Romans 12:21

Empathy - The capacity to understand or feel what another person is experiencing from within their frame of reference, that is, the capacity to place oneself in another's position.

My mother wounded me, but if I'm honest with myself I can say that she too was wounded.

Who wounded her?

_____

Take a moment to sit in the following truth **I was victimized by a victim**.

Hurt people hurt other people and wounded people wound other people.

SELAH
(Pause and calmly think about that)

(When I think of my mother, I see her wounded in the following areas)
*
*
*
*
*

Pray this prayer with me:

Father, only you understand how much I've been hurt by this person. I don't want to carry the pain for another second. I don't want to be a bitter person. But I need your grace and the power of the cross to release my hurt and to forgive those who've hurt me. This is the turning point. First, I need to experience your forgiveness. You know all the ways I've hurt others, and I'm so sorry for my sins. Jesus, thank you for dying for me. I accept your grace and forgiveness, and I need it daily. Today I'm turning to you, and I'm choosing to forgive the way you have forgiven me. Every time the memory comes back, I'll forgive that person again until the pain is gone. Heal my heart with your grace. In Jesus' name. Amen.

Doing The Work:

For the next seven days chose a consistent time of day to pray for your mother regarding the above listed identified areas of her wounding, holding empathy in your heart for how she sustained those wounds.

Week Two

---♡♡ ♡ ♡♡---

Open the Eyes of My heart Lord
Ephesians 1:18

Looking at the wounds inflicted on my mother makes me feel _____ **FOR** her

Looking at her wounds makes me feel
_____ **ABOUT** her

If I could heal **ONE** area of my mother's wounding it would be/would've been

_____
_____

The absence of that one wound may have freed her to be

_____
_____

Because she had **THAT** wound, she was/is

_____
_____
_____

And as a result, I experience/experienced her to be_____

_____
_____

The wound my mother carries/carried robbed her of

_____
_____ knowing that leaves me
FEELING:_____

_____
_____

THINKING:

_____
_____
_____

BELIEVING:

_____
_____
_____

My mother deserved

_____
_____
_____

Instead, she received

_____
_____
_____

Knowing that leaves me **FEELING**:

_____
_____
_____

THINKING:

_____
_____
_____

BELIEVING:

_____
_____
_____

Doing The Work:

For the next seven days chose a consistent time of day to pray for your mother holding sympathy in your heart for all that she lost, missed out on, never achieved or experienced.

Capacity: The potential or suitability for holding, storing or accommodating. An individual's mental or physical ability, aptitude or skill.

As a result of my mother being wounded, she wasn't/isn't able to meet the following needs that I **HAD/HAVE**

*
*
*
*

Realizing that she was/is **UNABLE** to meet my needs leaves me

FEELING:

_____

_____

_____

THINKING:

_____

_____

_____

BELIEVING:

_____

_____

_____

I **DO**_____ **DON'T**_____ believe my mother would have meet my need **IF** she **COULD**.

As a result of her being unable to meet my need/needs I experienced the following:

_____

_____

_____

SELAH
(Pause and calmly think about that)

Doing The Work:

For the next seven days chose a consistent time of day to acknowledge and accept your mother's actual level of capacity while praying for the strength, grace and ability to release her from expectations she was **_never_** equipped to meet.

Week Three

·♡· ♡ ·♡·

The Reciprocity of Forgiveness
Ephesians 4:32

Forgiveness - The intentional decision of releasing someone from an *emotional debt* that they **DON'T** have the ability to repay. Releasing them frees us from the burden of carrying an expectation that could **NEVER** be met.

Emotional debts are created by the absence of fundamental things and experiences that are (a) not tangible (b) beyond value (c) irreplaceable and (d) unable to be duplicated.

What emotional debts are you currently carrying?
 *
 *
 *
 *

To date, what **HAS BEEN** the cost of carrying the above listed debts?
 *
 *
 *
 *

Is this a cost you can continue to pay?
_____
_____
_____

What will be the **ULTIMATE** cost of **CONTINUING** to carry these debts?
_____
_____
_____

Is that a chance you're willing to take?

_____

_____

_____

Why or why not?

_____

_____

_____

What do you have to lose?

_____

_____

_____

*People (who are mentally and emotionally healthy) with something to LOSE don't gamble (with things they value)

SELAH
(Pause and calmly think about that)

Doing The Work:

For the next seven days chose a consistent time of day to really meditate on and grasp the magnitude of the emotional weight that you've been carrying along with the pain and chaos it's caused you.

In your prayer time this week, invite Jesus into that pain remembering his fatherly command that you cast ALL of your burdens and cares on him, allowing him to carry them simply because he cares for you. "*Pour out all your worries and stress upon him and leave them there, for he always tenderly cares for you*" **Peter 5:7 (TPT)**

Week Four

❤❤ ♥ ❤❤

Give To Get, Get To Give
Matthew 6:15

Forgive – Probably the only seven letter word powerful enough to stunt mental and emotional growth, sever relationships, preempt destines, induce anxiety and trigger pride all while stroking egos. "To forgive" means a lot of different things to a lot of different people and sometimes if we're not careful depending on the posturing of our hearts and the level of trauma and betrayal experienced the definition can become fluid as we actively engage protective shields and defense mechanisms.

Because the ability and willingness to forgive is a key component in this journey towards healing and recovery, it's import that we take a little time to look at what forgiving **is** and what forgiving is **not**. Many of us, myself included have forgone healing in the past simply because we were unwilling to forgive, we didn't know how to forgive, or we simply didn't understand what it meant to forgive in its proper context.

So, let's start with what forgiveness is **NOT**:
- Forgiving is **NOT** forgetting. Forgiving someone or something does not come with an automatic side of amnesia. A lot of people get stuck right here despite their desire and intention to forgive; when after going through their rituals and motions to forgive they find themselves still plagued by the memories of what happened, and the pain associated with their negative emotions. Not only is "forgiving & forgetting" unrealistic, it's not wise! If you forget what

happened and how it happened how can you protect yourself from being violated and hurt the exact same way in the future? Which brings me to my next point!

- Forgiving is **NOT** being open to continuing relationships and contacts with the people who hurt us the same way as before. In fact, we are urged and encouraged to use wisdom and employ God authorized boundaries.
- Forgiving is **NOT** a pardon. Forgiveness doesn't excuse the bad behavior of the person or persons who hurt you; forgiveness, however, prevents their behavior from destroying your heart
- Forgiving **IS** making a conscious decision **NOT** to carry the memories, the pain and the negative emotions associated with the violation forward into your future.
- Forgiving **IS** intentionally releasing someone from having to pay the penalty for their offense in light of the fact that we too have been and will be in need of forgiveness at some point in our lives.
- Forgiving **IS** releasing someone from an emotional debt they could **NEVER** repay because they could never do enough, be enough, give enough or say enough. Simply put, we release them from the penalty they could never satisfy.

Practicing forgiveness breaks the "Cycle of Offense"

Grace – Is the love and mercy given to us by God because he desires for us to have it, not necessarily because of anything we have done to earn or deserve it.

We forgive simply because we **WERE**, we **ARE,** and we **WILL** (at some time in the real near future) be in need of forgiveness. So, we give to others that which we have so freely received in the past and will expect in the future, **GRACE**.

Matthew 6:14-15 The Passion Translation (TPT)
14 *"And when you pray, make sure you forgive the faults of others so that your Father in heaven will also forgive you. * 15 *But if you withhold forgiveness from others, your Father withholds forgiveness from you."*

Mirror Check Moment

❦ ♡ ♡ ❦ ♡ ♡ ❦

When I'm completely honest with myself, there is one specific time when I can vulnerably say "I blew it". I (Insert appropriate offense) _____

_____. The moment I realized what I had done, how it had been received and the damage it caused,   I felt_____

_____because_____

_____. (Insert name of person who forgave you) _____forgave me even though I didn't deserve it. I am grateful because_____

_____

_____and   what   that experience   taught   me was_____

_____

_____

_____

As a result of that experience, I have grown in the following ways:
   *
   *
   *
   *

We give to others what we so richly received but did not deserve
Romans 5:6-8 The Passion Translation (TPT)

6 For when the time was right, the Anointed One came and died to demonstrate his love for sinners who were entirely helpless, weak, and powerless to save themselves. 7 Now, who of us would dare to die for the sake of a wicked person?[a] We can all understand if someone was willing to die for a truly noble person. 8 But Christ proved God's passionate love for us by dying in our place while we were still lost and ungodly! noble person. 8 But Christ proved God's passionate love for us by dying in our place while we were still lost and ungodly!

SELAH
(Pause and calmly think about that)

Doing The Work:

For the next seven days chose a consistent time to worship God through prayer and meditation thanking him for all of the times YOU'VE received his grace, mercy and forgiveness: along with the grace, mercy and forgiveness of others.

Week Five

— ♡ ♡ ♡ ♡ ♡ —

Choose Love
Proverbs 17:9

As I remind myself that forgiveness is a choice and not a feeling, I choose to forgive my mother for:

*
*
*
*

My forgiveness towards my mother **WILL** look like:

_____
_____
_____

And feel like:

_____
_____
_____

My forgiveness towards my mother will **NOT** look like:

_____
_____
_____

And it will **NOT** feel like:

_____
_____
_____

My forgiveness is a gift I freely give to myself & my mother.

Pray this prayer with me:

—— ♡ ♡ ♡ ♡ ♡ ——

Loving and gracious Father, in You we have redemption through Jesus' blood, the forgiveness of sins, in accordance with the riches of Your grace that You lavished on us with all wisdom and understanding (Ephesians 1:7-8). Lord, you are compassionate and gracious, slow to anger and abounding in love. You do not harbor Your anger forever and You do not treat us as our sins deserve. For as high as the heavens are above the earth, so great is Your love for those who fear You; as far as the east is from the west, so far have You removed our transgressions from us (Psalm 103:8-12). The depth of Your unending mercy and love is overwhelming. Thank you, Jesus, for enduring great pain and sacrifice so that our sins can be forgiven. Your death was the ultimate expression of Your love for us.

Humanly, I lack the ability to love and offer grace as You do, but the promise of Your Spirit living in me gives me hope. I confess my hard-hearted tendency to harbor bitterness, anger and un-forgiveness. I pray that out of Your glorious riches You would strengthen me with power through Your Spirit in my inner being.

Lord Jesus, in faith I ask that You establish Your presence in my heart. I need to be filled completely with You in order to experience Your power in a way that allows me to understand how wide and long and high and deep Your love is. I want to practically experience the love of Christ – the love that is beyond human understanding – so that I may be filled completely with all the fullness of You (Ephesians 3:16-19). Thank you for the hope I have in You! Because You live in me, I can be a grace-filled, loving person who forgives with generous mercy (1 John 4:12-13).

Doing The Work:

As we go into prayer this week, we hold in our hearts that forgiveness is a choice based upon a decision **NOT** a feeling. For the next seven days chose a consistent time of day to worship God through prayer and meditation thanking him for a tender heart filled with empathy, compassion and forgiveness for those who have ever hurt, betrayed, abandoned and abused you including your mother.

Week Six

The Price I've Paid
Galatians 6:8

The emotional weigh that I have carried has caused me to miss out on:

_____

_____

_____

To lose:

_____

_____

_____

To abandon:

_____

_____

_____

And to experience:

_____

_____

_____

Doing The Work:

During your prayer time this week, be intentional about being vulnerable before God your father; pour-out your heart to him about the experienced physical, mental and emotional cost of your wounding and the toll it's taken on you. Invite him into whatever pain you feel with the acknowledgement and then thank him for being with you even at your lowest moments when you felt like you were all alone.

"And never forget that I am with you every day, even to the completion of this age."[b] Matthew 28:20 (TPT)

Week Seven

— ♡ ♡ ♡ ♡ ♡ —

Manifesting God's Way
Proverbs 23:7

I Deserve...

Direction	Proverbs 3:5-6
Sound Rest	Matthew 11:28-30
Unconditional Love	John 3:16
Forgiveness	Romans 8:1
Hope	Romans 8:28
Wisdom	I Corinthians 1:30
Provision	2 Corinthians 9:8
Grace	2 Corinthians 12:9
Ability	Philippians 4:13
Resources	Philippians 4:19
Courage	2 Timothy 1:7
Companionship	Hebrews 13:5

As I embrace God's promises and plans for my life, I embrace hope for my future; and as an act of faith, I cast vision for my life!

I deserve (Actively list the self-identified things that you deserve):
*
*
*
*

I will achieve:
*
*
*
*

I will have:
*
*
*
*

I will conquer:
*
*
*
*

Doing The Work:

For the next seven days chose a consistent time to meet God in prayer and focus your worship on gratitude for all of the hope and potential of your future! Thank him for all that you have overcame and survived. Encourage yourself with the reminder that not only are you still standing but you're standing with the audacity to hope, dream, plan and command your future!!

Week Eight

♡ ♡ ♡ ♡ ♡

The Great Exchange!
GPS Location = The Foot of the Cross

Destination Details: It is here under the banner of grace we legally exchange joy for sadness, strength for weakness and wounds for healing. Before you move further into this week, meditate on each of the scriptures below as you contemplate all that you've exchanged in weeks one through seven and what you still have that you'd like to get rid of!

- For I am the Lord who heals you. − Exodus 15:26 (NLT)

- He heals the brokenhearted and bandages their wounds. − Psalm 147:2 (NLT)

- Then Jesus said, "Come to me, all of you who are weary and carry heavy burdens, and I will give you rest. Take my yoke upon you. Let me teach you, because I am humble and gentle at heart, and you will find rest for your souls." − Matthew 11:28-29 (NLT)

Pray this prayer with me:

With a heart full of gratitude, I embrace all that God has done to give me access to healing for my mind, my body and my soul. As a sign of faith, I enter into partnership with Him to receive the **FULL**

benefits afforded to me by His finished work on the cross.

Just like I chose to forgive; I chose to be healed, to be happy and to be whole!

As you get started on your journey towards healing here are some Practical Steps to help you get started:

LETTING GO OF REJECTION
The feeling of rejection toys with your natural need to belong and feel apart and is so distressing that rejection actually activates the same pathways in your brain as physical pain, which is one reason why it hurts so much. Unresolved rejection can interfere with your cognitive ability to think, recall memories and make decisions. Releasing the weight of rejection enhances your mental and emotional health and wellbeing

AVOID RUMINATING
When you ruminate, or brood, over a past hurt or event, the memories you replay in your mind become increasingly distressing and strong which can lead to even more anger – without providing any new insights. Now ruminating is different from reflecting. Reflecting on a painful event can help you to reach an understanding, assess areas for growth and development and bring closure. Ruminating however, increases your stress levels, and can actually be addictive.

BE COMMITTED TO TURNING FAILURE INTO SOMETHING POSITIVE

After a traumatic incident or event, we're all presented with a choice to become bitter or to become better. If you allow yourself to feel helpless after an event or blame it on your lack of ability or bad luck, it's likely to lower your self-esteem. Taking ownership of someone else's bad behavior that harmed you is just as detrimental to your mental and emotional health. Looking for ways and committing yourself to becoming better because of what you survived is a healthier path towards empowerment, healing and growth.

MAKE SURE GUILT REMAINS A USEFUL EMOTION

Guilt can be beneficial in that it can stop you from doing something that may harm yourself or someone else. But guilt that lingers or is excessive can be debilitating; it can impair your ability to focus and enjoy life.

If you still feel guilty after apologizing for an offense or wrongdoing that you committed, circle back to make sure that you have expressed empathy where appropriate and conveyed that you understand the impact your actions had on others Those actions will go a long way towards achieving authentic forgiveness and relief of your guilty feelings.

USE POSITIVE SELF AFFIRMATIONS TO COMBAT LOW SELF-ESTEEM

While *positive* affirmations are excellent tools for emotional health, if they fall outside the boundaries of your beliefs, they may be ineffective. This may be the case for people with low self-esteem, for whom *self*-affirmations may be more useful. Self-affirmations, such as "I have a great work ethic," can help to reinforce positive qualities you believe you have, as can making a list of your best qualities.

BE AN OPTOMIST
Looking on the bright side increases your ability to experience happiness in your day-to-day life while helping you cope more effectively with stress.

HAVE HOPE
Having hope allows you to see the light at the end of the tunnel, helping you push through even dark, challenging times. Accomplishing goals, even small ones, can help you to build your hope quotient.

ACCEPT YOURSELF
Critical comments, remarks and thoughts about yourself will cloud your mind with negativity and foster increased levels of stress. Seek out and embrace the positive traits of yourself and your life and avoid measuring your own worth by comparing yourself to those around you.

STAY CONNECTED
Having loving and supportive relationships helps you feel connected and accepted and promote a more positive mood. Intimate relationships help meet your emotional needs, so make it a point to

reach out to others to develop and nurture these relationships in your life.

COUNT YOUR BLESSINGS! NAME THEM ONE BY ONE
People who are thankful for what they have are better able to cope with stress, have more positive emotions, and are better able to reach their goals. The best way to harness the positive power of gratitude is to keep a gratitude journal or list, where you actively write down exactly what you're grateful for each day. Doing so has been linked to happier moods, greater optimism and even better physical health.

FIND YOUR PURPOSE AND YOUR MEANING
When you have a purpose or goal that you're striving for, your life will take on a new meaning that supports your mental and emotional well-being. If you're not sure what your purpose is, first pray about it, then begin to explore your natural talents and interests to help find it. Don't be afraid to try new things or things you've always wanted to do. Your purpose may be wrapped in a passion that you've been too reluctant to explore.

MASTER YOUR ENVIRONMENT
When you have mastery over your environment, you've learned how to best modify your unique circumstances for the most emotional balance, which leads to feelings of pride and success. Mastery entails using skills such as time management and prioritization along with believing in your ability to handle whatever life throws your way.

My dear brothers and sisters, what good is it if someone claims to have faith but demonstrates no good works to prove it? How could this kind of faith save anyone? [15] For example, if a brother or sister in the faith is poorly clothed and hungry [16] and you leave them saying, "Good-bye. I hope you stay warm and have plenty to eat," but you don't provide them with a coat or even a cup of soup, what good is your faith? [17] So then faith that doesn't involve action is phony. James 2:14-17

As a sign of faith and accountability, I will commit to taking the following steps towards healing from the inside out:

*
*
*
*

Accountability

Accountability
Noun
ac·count·abil·i·ty | \ ə-ˌkauṅ-tə-ˈbi-lə-tē \
:the quality or state of being accountable especially an obligation or willingness to accept responsibility or to account for one's actions

Christian accountability involves coming alongside someone you trust, someone grounded in their faith who will meet with you, listen to you, encourage you, and counsel you in your walk with the Lord — which always involves and includes our battle with sin. Accountability is a spiritual practice grounded in a connection that is forged through relationship, trust, emotional vulnerability, and the ups and downs of our spiritual walk and life.

The Benefits of Having an Accountability Partner
In 1 Corinthians chapter 12, we read that Christians are all part of the same body - the body of Christ - and each member needs or belongs to the other. This Scripture suggests the importance of strong accountability between Believers. It is important for every Believer to have at least one other person in which to confide, pray with, listen to, and encourage. Accountability partners can help by praying for their friends and watching out for them when they know that their friends have certain proclivities and vulnerabilities.

Brothers and sisters, if someone is caught in a sin, you who live by the Spirit should restore that person gently. But watch yourselves, or you also may be tempted. 2 Carry each other's burdens, and in this way, you will fulfill the law of Christ. Galatians 6:1-2

1. **Our perspective keeps us from seeing ourselves as we truly are**. We as people are often not so good at judging ourselves correctly. When evaluating ourselves we have a tendency to be either to strong, to harsh, too lenient or too permissive. Godly accountability partners are more objective in dealing with us and become a great assist as we move to line our lives up against God's standards and will for our lives.

Week Nine

— ♡ ♡ ❤ ♡ ♡ —

Use Your Lifeline
Proverbs 17:17

AFFIRM YOURSELF WITH THE FOLLOWING AFFIRMATION:

The only way I loose is if I quit, and quitting is not an option!

I have identified the following person _____ to support me along this healing journey and to hold me accountable to stay the course of the commitments I've made. As an act of good faith, I will share with them where I am, where I'm going (My Goal) and how I intend to get there (My commitment steps towards healing listed above).

Today's date is _____. I will have the conversation referenced above on or before (Enter a date within the next seven days) _____. After our initial conversation I will commit to checking in with them (enter a frequency time period NOT to exceed 14 days, i.e.: Once a week, every Tuesday or every other Monday)

_____

_____.

My ask of them will be to support me in the following ways:
- *
- *
- *
- *

In return, I will submit myself to their accountability in the following ways:

*

*

*

*

Doing The Work:

Over the next seven days in your daily prayer time with God ask him for the courage to be vulnerable and the grace needed to submit to godly accountability. Initiate contact with your identified accountability partner and share with them your identified steps towards healing. Share your support needs with them and ask them to partner with you. Upon acceptance share your commitment to accountability and the steps that you've outlined to demonstrate your commitment to the process.

Week Ten

— ♡ ♡ ♡ ♡ ♡ —

My Last Will & Testament

Proverbs 13:22

MY HEALING IS THE INHERITANCE OF MY CHILDREN & MY CHILDREN'S CHILDREN

As I intentionally embark upon this journey towards healing I do it as a gift to my children & grandchild listed below:

*   *
*   *
*   *
*   *
*   *

I embark upon this journey to intentionally break the cycle of passing down wounds and patterns of dysfunction to the offspring of this family. I AM doing the work because my children deserve:
   *
   *
   *
   *

I want them to have:
   *
   *
   *
   *

Now close your eyes, picture what that looks like. Now describe what you see:

_____
_____
_____
_____
_____

As I hold that vision in my heart for my children and grandchildren:

I **FEEL**:

_____
_____
_____
_____

I **THINK**:

_____
_____
_____
_____

I **BELIEVE**:

_____
_____
_____
_____

I am **WILLING TO**:

_____
_____
_____
_____

I am **COMMITTED TO**:

_____
_____
_____
_____

Doing The Work:

In your prayer time this week acknowledge God your father as a Good, Good Father! Thank him for the countless times and ways that he's clothed you during this process with his loving kindness. Think about all that he's done for and through you and as your worship him for who he is, thank him for giving you the ability to have the same parenting qualities that he demonstrates towards you. Thank him for the opportunity and ability to be a parent after his own heart. Thank him for your children and grandchildren. Thank him for their future and expected end. Began to vision cast in prayer all that your heart holds and desire for your offspring and then thank God for it not only coming to pass but also that all future generations will know and worship him as both Lord and Savior!

Week Eleven

$\heartsuit\ \heartsuit\ \heartsuit\ \heartsuit\ \heartsuit$

Failure to Plan = Planning to Fail

Proverbs 21:5

Today's date is:

_____

Get your phone and set the following reminders:
         *2 weeks _____ (insert
that date and designated time)
         *4weeks_____
(insert that date and designated time)
         *6weeks_____
(insert that date and designated time)

On each of the above referenced dates return to
this workbook for the following status update and
check-in.

2 WEEK STATUS UPDATE & CHECK-IN

Today I feel:

_____
_____
_____
_____
_____
_____

Over the last two weeks I have honored my
commitments in the following ways:
         *
         *
         *
         *
And as a result, I have **LEARNED**:

_____
_____

_____

_____

_____

I have **GROWN** in the following way:

_____

_____

_____

_____

_____

And as a result I have **CHANGED** in the following way:

_____

_____

_____

_____

_____

I know that I am getting better because: _____

_____

_____

_____

_____

_____

Two things that I am most proud of are:

_____

_____

_____

_____

_____

_____

Looking back over the last two weeks, if I could do one thing differently it would've been:

_____

_____

_____

_____

_____

_____

My strengths over the last two weeks were:

_____

_____

_____

_____

_____

My weaknesses over the last two weeks were:

_____

_____

_____

_____

_____

My identified focus area for the next two weeks will be:

_____

_____

_____

_____

_____

Week Twelve

—◦♡ ♡ ◦—

Celebrating the WINS in Me

Romans 8:37

4 WEEK STATUS UPDATE & CHECK-IN

Today I feel:

_____
_____
_____
_____
_____
_____

Over the last two weeks I have honored my commitments in the following ways:

    *

    *

    *

    *

And as a result, I have **LEARNED**:

_____
_____
_____
_____
_____

I have **GROWN** in the following way:

_____
_____

_____

_____

_____

_____

And as a result I have **CHANGED** in the following way:

_____

_____

_____

_____

_____

_____

I know that I am getting better because: _____

_____

_____

_____

_____

_____

_____

Two things that I am most proud of are:

_____

_____

_____

_____

_____

_____

Looking back over the last two weeks, if I could do
one thing differently it would've been:

_____

_____

_____

_____

_____

_____

My strengths over the last two weeks were:

_____

_____

_____

_____

My weaknesses over the last two weeks were:

_____

_____

_____

_____

_____

My identified focus area for the next two weeks
will be:

_____

_____

_____

_____

_____

Week Thirteen

— ♡ ♡ ♡ ♡ ♡ —

Claim Your Healing

Revelations 12:11

6 WEEK STATUS UPDATE & CHECK-IN

Today I feel:

_____

_____

_____

_____

_____

_____

Over the last two weeks I have honored my commitments in the following ways:

    *

    *

    *

    *

And as a result, I have **LEARNED**:

_____

_____

_____

_____

_____

I have **GROWN** in the following way:

_____
_____
_____
_____
_____
_____

And as a result I have **CHANGED** in the following way:

_____
_____
_____
_____
_____
_____

I know that I am getting better because: _____

_____
_____
_____
_____
_____

Two things that I am most proud of are:

_____

_____

_____

_____

_____

_____

Looking back over the last two weeks, if I could do one thing differently it would've been:

_____

_____

_____

_____

_____

_____

My strengths over the last two weeks were:

_____

_____

_____

_____

_____

My weaknesses over the last two weeks were:

_____

_____

_____

_____

_____

My identified focus area for the next two weeks will be:

_____

_____

_____

_____

_____

Congratulations!

Oh, my goodness you did it!! Can you believe it? I am incredibly proud of you because this was by no means an easy task! So, not only am I congratulating you on seeing this through, I am also welcoming you into what I pray will be the best years of your life! A life free of carrying around painful emotional baggage and the scent of its residue. My hope is that you have gained better insight into who your wounder was and how even they themselves came to be wounded; and that, that knowing nurtured a sense of empathy within you that not only freed you but, in your eyes, freed them as well.

A huge part of the work we did focused on our willingness and ability to pray for those who despitefully used and abused us *Matthew 5:44*. My hope is that by now, you have a testimony that mirrors the one proclaimed by Job, that God turned his captivity when he prayed for his friends; ushering him into a season described as being greater than any season he'd ever known before! *Job 42:10*.

While this phase of the work is complete, the process of maintaining emotional health, balance and wellbeing is a lifelong work; so, stay active, stay focused and stay vigilant of encounters and experiences that profoundly impact you to the point of wounding. Don't let it linger, don't allow it to fester; instead, acknowledge it, identify it, explore it, process it, make a decision and then let it go! The sustainability and the quality of your future and the inheritance of your children and the future generations of your bloodline is counting on it!

God Bless You

Sabrina

References

Diehl, Steve & Becky. 2010. Developing a Lifestyle of Forgiveness – A Personal and Small Group Study Guide to Help You Experience Healing, Freedom and Loving Relationships. Publisher

https://www.elephantjournal.com/2016/05/5-tools-for-healing-our-mother-wounds/

https://www.pixielighthorse.com/transforming-the-mother-wound/

https://www.fromhispresence.com/how-to-heal-from-mother-wounds/

https://www.crosswalk.com/devotionals/your-daily-prayer/a-prayer-for-forgiving-those-who-hurt-you-your-daily-prayer-october-3-2016.html

https://melany-oliver.com/3-ways-you-avoid-your-emotional-wounds/

About the Author

――✦―――♡ ♡ ♡ ♡ ♡――――✦――

Sabrina is a Licensed Clinical Social Worker with 20 years of social service experience working with children, their families and the vulnerable adult population. As a result of being raised in the Christian Community of the Bay Area and living in the community in which she serves Sabrina has developed a rich sense of cultural competency that has allowed her to work successfully with children and families of various ages, stages and backgrounds both professionally and spiritually. She specializes in working with adolescent girls and families dealing with trauma and transition. Sabrina has a special interest in providing guidance and support to teens and young adults as they transition into the next phase of their lives.

Sabrina earned her Master's degree in Social Work at California State University East Bay where she specialized in Adolescent Development and Children, Youth & Families; and she pursued her licensing hours at the Child Therapy Institute of Marin. By day, she works as a Licensed Clinical Therapist for one of the largest health care providers in Northern California and during the evening she can be found cultivating her therapeutic practice and coaching parents via parenting classes and seminar style trainings throughout Contra Costa County.

When not pursuing professional goals, Sabrina can be found worshipping and serving joyfully in the capacity of Ministry Coach at Praise Fellowship Bible Church of Richmond, California under the leadership of Senior Pastor, William Coleman, III, where she has been a member since 2009. She is the host of the popular radio show "High Tea with Bri" and she is a regular "Guest" co-host on the Stellar Nominated radio show "Shop Talk" both airing weekly on FreedemRadio.com. To round out her many accomplishments Sabrina is a proud member of the illustrious Delta Sigma Theta Sorority, Inc.

She is the proud mother of two adult daughters and Yaya to two beautiful grandchildren.

Simply put, Sabrina is a lover of God and people! She is known for her trademark smile and quirky sense of humor; guided by the principle of Proverbs 17:22 "A merry heart doeth good like medicine; but a broken spirit dries up the bones". Sabrina finds a way to infuse love and laughter into her professional and ministry capacities making her a sought-after therapist, speaker, program host and radio personality.

Made in the USA
Middletown, DE
19 October 2022